Notes On The Birds Of Fort Sherman, Idaho

James Cushing Merrill

In the interest of creating a more extensive selection of rare historical book reprints, we have chosen to reproduce this title even though it may possibly have occasional imperfections such as missing and blurred pages, missing text, poor pictures, markings, dark backgrounds and other reproduction issues beyond our control. Because this work is culturally important, we have made it available as a part of our commitment to protecting, preserving and promoting the world's literature. Thank you for your understanding.

NOTES ON THE BIRDS OF FORT SHERMAN, IDAHO.

BY J. C. MERRILL,

Major and Surgeon, U. S. Army.

FORT SHERMAN is situated in the northern part of the State of Idaho in latitude 47° 40', longitude 116° 30', and at an elevation of a little less than two thousand feet. The Idaho-Montana boundary line, formed here by the divide of the Bitterroot Mountains, is about seventy miles distant due east; that of Idaho-Washington is about eleven miles west, and that of British Columbia about ninety-five miles north.

The fort is on the northern shore of the northwestern arm of Lake Coeur d'Alêne, in the angle between the lake shore and the head of Spokane River, which is the outlet of the lake and empties into the Columbia about seventy-five miles north of west from the lake. The latter is nearly twenty-four miles in length, comparatively narrow in most parts, and its general trend is north and south. The Coeur d'Alêne Mountains, north and east of the lake, are a continuation of the Bitterroot range; in them arises the Coeur d'Alêne River, flowing into the southern end of the lake, and, still further south, the St. Joseph River forms the other principal tributary. The hills — they can hardly be called mountains — that encircle the lake are covered to the shores with a thick growth of pines and firs of two or three species, with tamaracks scattered throughout. Where streams flow into the lake there are often flats of a few acres in extent, subject to overflow in the spring; here a growth of tules, water grasses, and willows, with a limited number of cottonwoods on the edges, form the only inviting spots for a considerable number of land birds that never from choice enter the surrounding pine forests, and a few marsh birds and Ducks also frequent them. A belt of cottonwoods extends along the Spokane River for some miles and affords a convenient route for many migrants. Except close along shore the northern part of the lake is very deep, and in the autumn most water birds soon find their way to the southern end where the marshy valley of the St. Joseph River offers congenial feeding and resting places. About every third winter the surface of the lake is frozen; as long as it is open a few Grebes, Gulls and Ducks remain, going to the always open Spokane River when forced to by the ice. A marsh of the character described is about a mile southwest of the fort and is sometimes referred to in this paper. About six miles to the north, a pine forest intervening, is the eastern end of the great Spokane prairie. Mica Peak, locally so-called, one of the highest mountains in the vicinity, is about eleven miles to the southwest, gradually rising from near the lake shore to a height of about three thousand feet above it; the summit is about a mile east of the Washington State line. Another and the true Mica Peak is about three miles further southwest; it is in Washington, and is a little higher than the Idaho peak of the same name.

In some respects the local climatic conditions resemble those of the Northern Cascade Range more nearly than those of any other part of the Rocky Mountains or its neighboring ranges in the United States. The winters usually are not severe and Chinook winds are frequent. The rainfall, including its equivalent in the heavy winter snowfall, is considerable and the large number of cloudy days adds to the faunal effect of the actual rain and snow. The avifauna is, as would be expected, essentially that of the Northern Rocky Mountains, but there is an element of Cascade Mountain forms, as shown by the presence of such species as *Xenopicus, Troglodytes hiemalis pacificus, Parus rufescens, Hesperocichla*, and others.

The little collecting that has been done in Idaho was chiefly in the southern and central parts of the State and has been well brought together by Dr. C. Hart Merriam in Number 5 of the 'North American Fauna' series of the Department of Agriculture.[1] This report enumerates 156 species and throws much light on the summer fauna of Southern and Central Idaho. The present paper may be considered as supplementing it as to the winter avifauna and that of the northern part of the State. Since the publication of Dr. Merriam's paper Prof. B. W. Evermann made a small collection in the Sawtooth range district in September, 1894, and has kindly allowed me to look over his MS. notes. Two male Pipilos, identified as probably *megalonyx*, is the first record of this species in Idaho.

The following observations were made from November, 1894, until December, 1896. One hundred and sixty-seven species are enumerated, of which fifty, to each of which an asterisk is prefixed, have not, so far as I am aware, been previously taken in Idaho. I desire to express my obligations to Mr. William Brewster for kindly identifying some of the species; his opinions are incorporated in the text.

* Æchmophorus occidentalis.— A single specimen taken.

* Colymbus holbœlii.— Resident but most common during migrations. A nearly completed nest was found in the marsh on May 18; when again visited on June 3 it contained four eggs, but was deserted, owing probably to the rapid fall of the lake level leaving it high and dry. The parents continued in the vicinity throughout the summer and probably bred again.

---

[1] One paper has been overlooked by Dr. Merriam in the preparation of his list. It has the somewhat misleading title of 'The Fauna of Montana Territory,' by J. G. Cooper, and may be found in the 'American Naturalist,' II, pp. 596-600; III, pp. 31-35; 73-84; also p. 224. The context shows that certain species were taken or observed in what is now the State of Idaho. Of such not included in the Merriam list are, to quote the names as given, *Falco columbarius, Turdus nævius, Sialia mexicana, Sciurus noveboracensis, Setophaga ruticilla, Sitta pygmæa, Parus rufescens, Curvirostra americana* var. *mexicana, Curvirostra leucoptera, Corvus caurinus, Columba fasciata, Ectopistes migratorius*. It may be remarked in regard to these species that the Water Thrush was undoubtedly the *notabilis* form; the Crossbill *L. curvirostra minor*, and the Crow *C. americanus*, and not what is now understood as *caurinus*. *Columba fasciata* was not satisfactorily identified.

Sciurus aurocapillus should also be added to the avifauna of Idaho, as Dr. Cooper states (Bull. N. O. C., II, 1877, p. 91) that it has been "recently recorded from Idaho." I do not know where this record is to be found.

Podilymbus podiceps.— Common on the lake in spring and autumn.

Urinator imber.— Resident and quite common except in winter.

*Larus argentatus smithsonianus.— Several taken on the lake during fall and winter.

*Larus delawarensis.— An adult taken January 6, and several young in September; not rare during winter. I saw no Gulls on the lake during summer.

*Larus philadelphia.— One taken and several seen in November.

A small white Tern breeds about the lake, but I did not succeed in procuring any specimens for positive identification.

Phalacrocorax dilophus cincinatus.— Several Cormorants, probably of this form, were seen on September 19.

*Merganser americanus.— Common during fall and winter.

Merganser serrator.— A single specimen taken.

*Lophodytes cucullatus.— The most abundant of the Mergansers, frequenting especially the rivers, and in the autumn collecting in flocks of forty and fifty individuals.

Anas boschas.— The most common Duck in this vicinity, a few remaining throughout the winter.

Anas americana.— During the latter part of September this is one of the most common Ducks in the marshes at the southern end of the lake.

Anas carolinensis.— Quite common, especially during the migrations.

Anas cyanoptera.— Rare. A female with several young two or three days old seen June 11.

Spatula clypeata.— Common. Said to have been unusually abundant in the autumn of 1894. About twenty-five were seen about the fort on June 1; they were mostly paired and had perhaps been driven out of the St. Joseph marshes, where they breed, by the unusually high water.

*Dafila acuta.— Common in migrations.

*Aix sponsa.— Common summer visitor, especially abundant at the southern end of the lake during the early autumn.

*Aythya collaris.— Seems to be more common than the other 'Bluebills,' one or both of which occur, but were not certainly identified.

*Clangula islandica.— Abundant throughout the winter. All the Goldeneyes seen by me were of this species, although the other doubtless occurs.

*Charitonetta albeola.— Common during winter.

*Histrionicus histrionicus.— Rare, but occasionally taken on the St. Joseph and Coeur d'Alêne Rivers.

*Erismatura jamaicensis.— Not uncommon in spring and autumn.

Branta canadensis.— Common in spring, rare in autumn. The most abundant species of Goose, especially on the prairie and at the southern end of the lake. I have seen them as early as February 22, although the middle of March is the more usual time of their arrival. A few pairs nest near the lake, but much less frequently than a few years ago, owing to the increase of settlers. Very few Geese are seen during the fall flight as at this season they, as well as many Ducks, pass south over the open prairie country about fifty miles west of the lake.

Hunters have told me that the White-fronted and Snow Geese are sometimes shot, but that they are decidedly rare.

Olor *sp.?* — In the spring Swans are sometimes quite common on the marshes bordering the rivers at the southern end of the lake and in the lake itself. I was unable to examine any specimens for identification.

* **Botaurus lentiginosus.** — Rather common in suitable localities about the lake.

Grus mexicana. — Not uncommon during the migrations, and a few pairs probably breed near the southern end of the lake.

Porzana carolina. — Not rare in the marshes; breeds.

Fulica americana. — Common, especially in autumn.

Phalaropus lobatus. — Occurs during the latter part of August and early in September on the lake, sometimes in great numbers, but passes through rapidly.

Recurvirostra americana. — A pair seen and one taken early in September.

Gallinago delicata. — Usually rather uncommon, but occurring in considerable numbers during the autumn of 1896. They appeared during the last week in August and were abundant until the middle of September, affording fine sport. A second flight of somewhat larger and darker birds appeared on October 22 and remained about two weeks, the last one being seen on November 5. I am inclined to think that the first flight was of birds breeding in the general vicinity, the second, of birds from more northern localities.

* **Macrorhamphus griseus.** — Five specimens, taken September 12 on the St. Joseph marshes, were decidedly of the eastern form.

Tringa maculata. — Common in 1896 from the last of August until early in October. Abundant on September 12, when about 125 were shot. Many were in flocks of considerable size, not a common habit with this species.

* **Tringa minutilla.** — Three taken August 15.

Ereunetes occidentalis. — One taken in company with the preceding.

Totanus melanoleucus. — A rather common fall migrant. One heard on June 20.

Totanus solitarius. — A young bird taken August 26.

* **Bartramia longicauda.** — Breeds not uncommonly on the prairie north of the fort. They begin to leave for the South about the twentieth of July.

Actitis macularia. — Common summer visitor. Several nests were found near the fort.

Numenius longirostris. — Not uncommon on the prairie, arriving during the latter part of March.

* **Squatarola squatarola.** — Four taken September 12 on the St. Joseph marshes.

* **Charadrius dominicus.**— Usually rare. A large flight passed through northern Idaho and eastern Washington from the 15th to 20th of September, 1896. This was so uncommon that the local papers had notices of their presence, with highly original accounts of the birds' usual haunts and habits.

Ægialitis vocifera.— A few pairs breed on the prairie near the Spokane River.

Dendragapus obscurus richardsonii.— Occasionally found about the fort, but more common a few miles away, where they are not hunted so much. Breeds from lake level to the tops of the surrounding mountains. On July 1, near the base of Mica Peak, a brood of nearly grown young was seen; the next day, just below the summit, a female with a brood of chicks was found; the latter at once scattered in the grass and the parent, to obtain a better view of what was going on, flew up and alighted on the pack of one of the mules.

Dendragapus franklinii.— In the autumn of 1894 about forty specimens of this beautiful Grouse were brought in for sale by a ranchman, who said that he killed them on Canfield's Butte, a high hill a short distance northeast of the fort. While hunting near the southern end of Lake Pend d'Oreille the settlers told me that the 'fool hen' was rather common in the surrounding woods, but I did not happen to see any.

Bonasa umbellus togata.— Exceedingly abundant, much more so than I have ever found any form of the Ruffed Grouse. Many are killed by ranchmen and others over dogs trained to tree the birds, and the local market is plentifully supplied. One man told me that he no longer cared for them on his own table, but that he still fed his dogs on them!

Pediocætes phasianellus columbianus.— Quite common in all suitable localities, particularly about ranches on the extensive prairie north of the fort. In the winter it penetrates into the pine woods for considerable distances, passing the nights and the greater portion of stormy days in the trees.

Zenaidura macroura.— Not common, but generally distributed in the vicinity.

Cathartes aura.— A few are seen at intervals during the summer, arriving about the middle of April and leaving in September.

Circus hudsonius.— Not uncommon in autumn.

Accipiter velox.— One taken May 15.

Accipiter atricapillus.— Rather common during the migrations and winter, and probably breeds, as I have taken a specimen as late as May 30. Especially abundant during the early part of the winter of 1896–97, many being killed, while attacking chickens, by ranchmen and others. It may be remarked that Snowy Owls were unusually common about the same time, and that a specimen of *Falco rusticolus* was shot at Spokane, Wash., about twenty-five miles distant.

Buteo swainsoni.— A young bird taken September 14.

*Archibuteo lagopus sancti-johannis.— Occasionally seen in early spring and late autumn.

Aquila chrysaëtos.— Occurs sparingly throughout the year.

Haliæetus leucocephalus.— A few pairs breed about the lake. An adult seen on February 5.

Falco mexicanus.— Rare; taken in September.

*Falco richardsonii.— Of a male taken August 20 Mr. Brewster remarks: "This specimen is unusually dark and richly colored," but the wing markings were typical of the species. A young female was taken October 1.

Falco sparverius deserticolus.— The Sparrow Hawk arrives early in April and is common by the 15th–20th; breeds. With the exception of this species and the Goshawk and Osprey, Hawks are remarkably scarce about Fort Sherman, although apparently there is an abundant supply of food at all seasons.

Pandion haliaëtus carolinensis.— First observed April 25 and frequently seen thereafter during the summer.

Asio wilsonianus.— A single specimen examined.

Asio accipitrinus.— This Owl is frequently flushed on the prairie and marshes in the autumn.

*Nyctala tengmalmi richardsoni. — Two fine specimens are in Mr. Shallis's local collection which were taken early in the spring of 1894 on the prairie about seven miles from the fort. These, and a third specimen brought to him some years ago, are the only ones Mr. Shallis has seen.

*Nyctala acadica.— A specimen taken January 19; its stomach contained two *Hesperomys*. During the spring its notes are frequently heard at night in the deep woods bordering the lake.

Megascops asio *subsp.?*— Screech Owls were occasionally heard in and about the fort, doubtless the *macfarlanei* form. They were quite rare, apparently.

Bubo virginianus subarcticus.

Bubo virginianus saturatus. — Both forms of the Great-horned Owl occur here commonly, and, judging from the specimens I have examined, in about equal numbers.

Nyctea nyctea.— Not uncommon in some winters, but irregular and uncertain. In December, 1896, there was a general migration of Snowy Owls into northern Idaho, Oregon and Washington and dozens were killed.

*Glaucidium gnoma.— Not uncommon and a resident.

*Coccyzus americanus occidentalis.— One seen July 30, 1895.

Ceryle alcyon.— Common during summer. A few pass the winter but most return from the South about the middle of April.

Dryobates villosus hyloscopus.— Abundant during winter, and more often seen at that season than all other Woodpeckers combined. Females were more common than males in the proportion of at least four or five to one. A series of specimens are of greater size than the usual average of this bird. Cabanis's Woodpecker is here very unsuspicious, in marked contrast to its behavior in some other regions. After the first of March they are much less common and they breed but sparingly near the fort. Two nests found June 15 contained young, a late date.

Dryobates pubescens homorus.—Rather uncommon resident, breeding sparingly. Specimens taken here differ from all of the recognized forms in some respects.

Xenopicus albolarvatus.—A rare resident.

Picoides arcticus.—A fairly common resident, especially on the higher parts of the hills, where in winter I have seen many nesting excavations undoubtedly made by this bird, which shows a marked partiality for locating them near the base of slender pine stubs. Mr. Brewster informs me that the bills of specimens taken at Fort Sherman are longer and slenderer than in eastern examples, but less so than in the series I took at Fort Klamath, Oregon.

* **Sphyrapicus varius nuchalis.**—A few pairs breed among the cottonwoods bordering the lake near its outlet and along the river.

Ceophlœus pileatus.—A rather common resident, more plentiful in the deep woods.

Melanerpes torquatus.—Arriving early in May, Lewis's Woodpecker soon becomes common and is generally distributed, breeding in cottonwoods as well as in pines.

Colaptes cafer.—Common summer visitor arriving late in March, though a few remain throughout the winter. Breeds from lake level up to the summit of Mica Peak. Dr. Allen, in the map accompanying his paper on the Flickers,[1] places northern Idaho in the habitat of *C. auratus cafer*, or *hybridus*, as it was formerly called; but all the specimens taken at Fort Sherman, both breeding and migrating birds, were pure *cafer*.

* **Chordeiles virginianus.**—Arriving about the first of June, few are seen until the 12th or 15th, when they suddenly become common, and so remain until early in August, when more arrive from the north. They are abundant until the end of the month, when most leave, a few stragglers being seen until the middle of September.

In regard to some skins collected here Mr. Brewster writes: "This series, as a whole, seems to me to be referable to *virginianus*, although two or three of the females have too much gray on the back and wings to be typical. The male, on the other hand, is a typical *virginianus*."

* **Chætura vauxii.**—This Swift arrives early in May and may be seen almost daily during the month, generally singly. About July 20 they again appear and pass rapidly to the south, though I have seen one as late as August 31. While none were observed during the breeding

---

[1] 'The North American Species of the Genus Colaptes,' etc. Bull. Am. Mus. Nat. Hist., IV, map facing p. 24.

season I have little doubt that some remain, as late in May I have watched them apparently breaking off dead twigs near the tops of high cottonwoods, though this may have been in play. This, and the western Montana record in Bendire's 'Life Histories' (Vol. II. p. 183), considerably extend to the eastward the known range of this species. I have frequently seen Swifts along the Yellowstone River in Montana but have been unable to secure any for identification.

Trochilus alexandri. — Fairly common late in May, especially about the low, lavender-colored blossoms of the camass. A few pairs remain to breed.

Selasphorus rufus. — A common spring migrant, probably breeding. Found most frequently about blossoms of cherry trees in the yards about the officers' quarters. I have rarely seen this Hummer outside the fort, or the other two within it.

Stellula calliope. — The most common of the Hummers at Fort Sherman, both during the spring migration and the nesting season, their arrival in both years coinciding with the first blossoming of the wild hawthorn.

A good many Hummers, probably of the three species, pass through to the south during the latter part of August.

Tyrannus tyrannus. — Arriving during the last week in May, the Kingbird at once becomes fairly common among the cottonwoods bordering the river, and in which it nests.

Tyrannus verticalis. — Rare; but a pair or two breed each year near the fort.

Contopus borealis. — Breeds sparingly at a height of several hundred feet above lake level.

Contopus richardsonii. — Very common, both in pine woods and in cottonwoods bordering the river.

Empidonax hammondi. — Northern Idaho must be near the center of abundance of this Flycatcher, and it is far more plentiful here than I have found it to be in Montana and Oregon. Arriving early in May, its habits here are somewhat peculiar, for it is as common among young cottonwoods and willows along the river and in and near swamps — just such places as *E. traillii* haunts — as in dry woods among pines, in which it is generally seen in the higher branches. It breeds in the latter situations, and I also took a good series of nests in young cottonwoods and aspens, some not more than two or three feet above the ground or water. When in pines the nest is usually thirty or forty feet from the ground, saddled on a horizontal dead branch several feet from the trunk, and is much like a *Contopus* nest. When placed in a young cottonwood the nest is more like that of *E. wrightii*, near the ground and generally against the trunk. I found Hammond's Flycatcher to be by no means as shy as other observers have noted; in fact, it is here one of the most common and, for an *Empidonax*, conspicuous of the summer visitors, its notes being heard almost everywhere. Of a number of sets of eggs collected at Fort Sherman none were entirely unspotted but a majority were marked at the larger end, more or less distinctly, with delicate light brown dots.

Empidonax wrightii. — Only a single specimen taken; this was on May 17.

* **Otocoris alpestris leucolæma.** — A typical female taken September 28, on the prairie. This was one of a number of Horned Larks collected on the same day and at the same place, all the others being of the next form.

* **Otocoris alpestris merrilli.** — Careful search failed to reveal the presence of either form of Horned Lark during the winter, though it is probable that *leucolæma* occasionally occurs about ranch yards at that season. The present one returns in March, and during spring and summer is very common on the prairie, but none were seen at any time about the post gardens and adjoining fields, apparently equally suited to their habits. When grouse shooting in August these Larks were often flushed in corn and potato fields on the prairie where they sought shelter from the intense heat of the sun. Later they are found in the open prairie, stubble or ploughed land, collecting in flocks of twenty, forty or more.

Referring to a series of skins collected here, Mr. Brewster writes: "Specimens from Fort Sherman appear to be referable to *O. a. merrilli* although they are not typical, having the dorsal streaking much less pronounced than in Klamath birds. The autumnal examples are also more olivaceous above than the latter."

Pica pica hudsonica. — Not uncommon in winter, a few individuals making daily visits to the back yards of the quarters and to the garbage pile a few hundred yards outside the fort. There was a decided increase in their numbers about the middle of February, but they were rarely seen after March, and none appear to breed near the fort.

Cyanocitta stelleri annectens. — Fairly common about the fort in spring and autumn, a few passing the winter. It does not appear to breed at lake level but several pairs were seen early in July on Mica Peak, first at an elevation of about 1500 feet above the lake and thence upward to the summit. These Jays are typical *annectens*.

Perisoreus canadensis capitalis. — Rather common resident. A pair was seen collecting building material for a nest in a young pine on April 17, near Hoodoo Lake, about forty miles from the fort, but I was unable to return to secure it.

Mr. Brewster informs me that some skins sent him were much darker than Colorado specimens and had the dark occipital band broader.

Corvus corax sinuatus. — Probably resident; seen occasionally during the winter.

Corvus americanus. — Common during the migrations, a few pairs breeding near the edge of the prairie.

Nucifraga columbiana. — Probably owing to the identity of their principal winter food this species and the Crossbill were coincidentally abundant during the winter of 1894-95, very rare during that of 1895-96, and again common during so much of the winter of 1896-97 as I was at the fort, these periods being marked by the abundance or failure of the crop of cones of a common pine, upon the seeds of which both species chiefly fed. At other seasons Clark's Nutcracker appeared irregularly, probably wandering down from the surrounding hills, as, early in July, I saw several families on the higher parts of Mica Peak. For the first time in my experience in the Northwest I found this usually shy and suspicious bird to be quite tame in winter, visiting the yards of the houses for such scraps as were to be found; and they were especially fond of pecking at bones left on the surface of the snow by dogs. Several were caught by cats and one by a soldier in his hands.

(To be concluded.)

[From 'THE AUK,' Vol. XV, No. 1, January, 1898.]

NOTES ON THE BIRDS OF FORT SHERMAN, IDAHO.

BY J. C. MERRILL,

Major and Surgeon, U. S. Army.

(*Concluded from Vol. XIV, p. 357.*)

NOTES ON THE BIRDS OF FORT SHERMAN, IDAHO.

BY J. C. MERRILL,

Major and Surgeon, U. S. Army.

(*Concluded from Vol. XIV, p. 357.*)

Dolichonyx oryzivorus.— The well-known song of the Bobolink was heard in July at a ranch on the St. Joseph River, and an old settler told me that the birds were quite common there each year.

Molothrus ater.— As in most parts of the Northwest, the Cowbird is rare at Fort Sherman. A single specimen only, a female, was taken May 25, 1896. Among the many nests of small birds examined none contained either egg or young of this parasite.

Agelaius phœniceus.— One of the first migrants to appear, as I have seen it on February 22. After remaining two or three weeks these early birds seem to pass on to the north and none are seen until about the first of May when others, apparently the birds nesting here, arrive. Breeds sparingly about the lake, more commonly on the Coeur d'Alêne and St. Joseph Rivers.

Sturnella magna neglecta.— Arriving early in March, the Meadowlark is very common during the summer. I found it nesting at the summit of Mica Peak.

Icterus bullocki.— Breeds sparingly in cottonwoods along the river, especially after it enters Spokane prairie.

Scolecophagus cyanocephalus.— A few pairs breed in bushes along the river bank near the fort. Occasionally a small flock may be seen about the stables throughout the winter.

Coccothraustes vespertinus montanus.— I am somewhat uncertain as to the true status of this species at Fort Sherman. Mr. Shallis, a local collector, informs me that it usually occurs from May to July and that it is absent during the rest of the year. In 1895 I did not observe any but Mr. Shallis, who knows the bird well, told me that he saw three small flocks about the middle of August. This Grosbeak was first seen by me on May 28, 1896, though their loud whistling notes had been heard a few days earlier. June 1 many were seen in pines and firs across the river, in twos and threes and in irregular flocks; they were restless, whistling constantly, and kept high up in the trees. Common during the next few days, they were scarce but not absent from about June 10 till early in July, when they were again common in small flocks, which at first consisted exclusively of males, joined soon after by females and young They were now quite tame, coming about the houses and feeding much on the ground, permitting a close approach. I was absent from July 29 until

August 19 and saw none after my return. It is probable that this bird is a common but irregular summer visitor, nesting in the high pines and firs in the hills surrounding the lake, to the borders of which many return as soon as the young are fledged.

Carpodacus cassini. — Arriving about the middle of April, this fine songster is one of the most abundant summer birds at Fort Sherman, breeding commonly about the houses as well as on the surrounding hills.

Loxia curvirostra minor. — As before stated, the occurrence of the Crossbill at Fort Sherman is irregular; they are sometimes as common and fearless as the English Sparrow. I have seen them in the fort every month in the year, but in summer most of them are in the neighboring hills. On warm bright days in February and March their pleasing song may be heard in every direction, and I have been informed that their nests with eggs have been found here in the former month, placed in tamaracks at a height of thirty or forty feet from the ground. The heavy pines and firs collect and shed the snow to a considerable extent, often leaving a bare spot around the base of the trunk while between scattered trees the snow may be one or two feet in depth. In these bare places, early in March, I have watched male and female Crossbills collect building material, both pine needles and dead grasses, a constant habit being to do this at a considerable distance from the nest for they always carried their loads out of sight, though I have watched them, for several hundred yards when the woods were open enough to permit this. During the latter part of summer there is a marked resumption of their song as heard in early spring. Mr. Brewster informs me that specimens taken here are typical of the former subspecies *bendirei*.

* **Leucosticte tephrocotis littoralis.** — There is a specimen in a small collection of birds in the local post office. Apparently an irregular fall and winter visitor, known to many of the settlers from its tameness and presence about farm yards. None were seen during the winters of 1894-95 and 1895-96, although careful search was made by myself and others. On November 3, 1896, a flock of about fifty was seen on a hillside near the fort. None were obtained, but they once flew very near to me and they were certainly not *L. atrata*, which Dr. Merriam found in the southern part of the State.

* **Acanthis linaria.** — A regular winter visitor, but varying greatly in its abundance. Their numbers are much increased about the middle of March by arrivals from the South. I have seen them as late as April 11.

Spinus tristis. — A fairly common summer resident.

Spinus pinus. — Resident. In summer it occurs quite commonly on Mica Peak, from about 1500 feet above the lake to the summit.

* **Plectrophenax nivalis.** — An irregular winter visitor, sometimes occurring on the prairies in large flocks.

* **Calcarius lapponicus.** — A single specimen taken November 13, 1896.

Poocætes gramineus confinis. — Breeds sparingly.

Ammodramus sandwichensis alaudinus. — Arriving early in May, it passes through in moderate numbers, a few remaining to breed on the prairie. In September and early in October it is very common, especially so on the marsh.

***Ammodramus leconteii.**— A specimen taken on the marsh September 28, 1896. It arose from tall marsh grass and alighted on a neighboring swamp willow, from which a hasty shot dropped it; great was my surprise to pick up a Leconte's Sparrow. I do not think it has previously been taken west of the Rocky Mountains. Careful search on several subsequent days in the same locality failed to reveal other specimens.

Zonotrichia leucophrys intermedia.— Fairly common in spring and fall.

Spizella monticola ochracea.— Rare in winter.

Spizella socialis arizonæ.— Arriving about the last week in April, this Sparrow is one of the commonest summer birds.

Junco hyemalis connectens.— Arrives during the last week of February or early in March, many returning from the north about the middle of September. On April 3 a small flock was observed near the top of a large pine tree; they were searching for insects near the ends of the branches, assuming the various attitudes of Titmice for which, although having watched them for some time, I mistook them until one was shot and picked up.

***Melospiza fasciata merrilli.**— This new subspecies[1] is a common summer visitor at Fort Sherman, frequenting the shores of the lake and inflowing rivers, and following the smaller streams up to their sources in the surrounding hills. Careful search during two winters failed to reveal the presence of this bird, yet I am inclined to think that a few do pass that season here in favorable localities; and that while the great majority certainly do leave on account of the great depth of snow, their migration is a short one to the southwest, where in eastern Washington and Oregon the snow fall is much less and food more easily obtained in winter. I have seen one as late as December 10, and have heard their song as early as the last week in February; by the middle of March they are fairly common. There is nothing in their notes or general habits to distinguish them from the Song Sparrows of other parts of the country, but their partiality to the immediate vicinity of water is very marked, and most of the nests found during the seasons of 1895 and 1896 were in bushes growing in water. In 1896, a cold, backward season, a female taken April 24 had deposited her eggs and was incubating; and on May 25 a brood of fully fledged young was seen.

All the nests I have found were above the ground, one reason for which is probably the great rise of water in the lake and rivers about nesting time, a rise that yearly destroys many nests of this and other low building species. Various kinds of bushes, and sometimes small trees, are selected as suitable building sites for the nests; sometimes in the dense top of a wild rose on the river bank; sometimes in

---

[1] See Auk, XIII, p. 46.

bushes growing in water; a favorite place is among the debris lodged in a bush during high water of the previous year, where the nest is admirably concealed and readily escapes notice. Two nests were found in young cottonwoods where a cluster of small branches grew out from the main trunk. The nests, in whatever situation, are unusually large for a Song Sparrow and composed chiefly of dead leaves and strips of cottonwood bark, deeply cupped and lined with finer materials of the same general kind. The thirty-two eggs collected appear to average a trifle larger than those of other subspecies of the Song Sparrow, and are more uniformly greenish in their general appearance. Two broods are raised; five is the usual number of eggs in the first, three or four in the second. As soon as the young are fledged these birds leave their nesting haunts along the river and are to be found among the willow thickets on the marsh.

*Passerella iliaca schistacea. — A rare migrant, taken in May.

Pipilo maculatus megalonyx. — Arriving in April, this bird is generally but sparingly distributed during the summer.

Zamelodia melanocephala. — Not uncommon. While examining a nest with eggs on June 25, the male alighted on the bush and sang almost continuously while I was there.

Passerina amœna. — Not common.

Piranga ludoviciana. — Arrive during the last week in May and are quite common among pines during the migration, though but few breed here. A nest found June 29 was in a small pine about thirty feet from the ground and about six feet from the trunk, on a branch so slender that it seemed as if the weight of the nest and sitting female would break it.

Petrochelidon lunifrons. — Common summer visitor, arriving about the last of April and leaving suddenly about the middle of August.

Chelidon erythrogaster. — Not observed about the fort or town during the breeding season but occasionally seen about ranches near the prairie.

*Tachycineta bicolor. — Arrive from the middle to the end of March, according to the season, and breed abundantly in cottonwood trees along the lake and river, forming quite a colony at the outlet of the lake.

Clivicola riparia. — Many seen July 16 on the Coeur d'Alêne River, the low banks of which in places were perforated by their excavations. Seen only during migrations at the fort.

Ampelis garrulus. — An irregular winter visitor, taken in January and March.

Ampelis cedrorum. — Arriving irregularly in April and May, the Cedar Bird becomes quite common by the end of the latter month and remains until about the 20th of August. Unlike my previous experience with this species in the West, it is here very tame. Several nests were found in thorn bushes at the edge of the river; these were essentially alike in construction and as compared with eastern ones, rather loose and bulky.

They were composed externally of light colored strips of bark and flood debris, among masses of which they were placed — as are many of those of the Song Sparrow — and very well concealed. They were lined with the long black fibrous moss so common on pine trees in this region, interspersed with a few blades of dry grass, rootlets, and broken pine needles. One nest was built in a cottonwood sapling, and its exterior much resembled a nest of Swainson's Thrush, for which I mistook it until I saw the eggs.

Lanius borealis. — Common in the fall, arriving early in November. A few remain throughout the winter.

*****Vireo olivaceus.** — An abundant summer visitor, arriving about the 20th of May, and frequenting cottonwood and aspen groves in company with the next species, which it much exceeds in numbers. Several nests were found, all within six feet of the ground, in bushes or young trees among larger cottonwoods, in which the birds were to be heard singing throughout the day.

Vireo gilvus. — Arrives in May in considerable numbers and breeds somewhat sparingly.

Vireo solitarius cassinii. — Arrives about the 10th of May and is soon common in pine woods, to which it shows a marked partiality; breeds in moderate numbers.

* **Helminthophila rubricapilla gutturalis.** — Not uncommon during May, the song of the male being frequently heard on the hillside across the river. Breeds.

* **Helminthophila celata lutescens.** — Several specimens taken in May.

Dendroica æstiva. — Abundant during the summer, arriving early in May. Of many nests examined the majority contained five eggs or young.

Dendroica auduboni. — Arriving about the middle of April, Audubon's Warbler slowly increases in numbers, and by the first of May is common. Many pass through during this month, but not in such numbers as I have seen in other parts of the Northwest, nor does it breed here very commonly. It was not more plentiful on Mica Peak than at lake level. Early in August the fall migration is noticeable and by the 10th is usually well marked, continuing until the end of September. Elsewhere I have found Audubon's Warbler very partial to coniferous trees, and nesting in them almost exclusively. Here a majority of the nests I found were in deciduous trees and bushes, generally but a few feet from the ground. One was in a small rose bush growing at the edge of a cut bank overhanging a road where wagons daily passed close to it. Such nests as were found here, while varying considerably as to exterior, agree in having a lining in which black horse hairs are conspicuous, and in which feathers are loosely attached, not well woven in as is usual in most small nests. Occasionally one was seen in deep woods by the roadside near where hay had been brushed off a load on a passing wagon; this was utilized for the entire nest except lining, making a conspicuous yellow object in the dark green fir or pine in which it was placed.

*Dendroica townsendi. — During the spring of 1895 I frequently heard the note of a Dendroica that I could not identify, though much time was devoted to this end. Two or three males were to be heard daily in their respective ranges, which were among large firs growing on the hillside across the river. They seemed to haunt exclusively the tops of these trees, flitting from one to another at such a height as to make their identification by sight impossible, and their capture a very difficult matter. They were active and restless, passing rapidly from tree to tree along the hillside for a few hundred yards and returning over the same route, this habit being observed at all hours of the day. The few shots obtained were at such distances as to be ineffectual. The birds were evidently nesting, the song gradually diminishing in frequency until the end of June when it ceased.

On May 21, 1896, it was again heard and almost daily subsequently. At last, on June 2, a lucky shot brought down a fine male *D. townsendi* which, although not in the act of singing when shot, is, I have little doubt the author of the song. This usually consists of five notes — deé deé deé — dĕ dĕ all, especially the first three, uttered in the peculiar harsh drawl of *D. virens*. Later in the season this song changes somewhat at times — at least I think that both are uttered by the same species — and on June 29, I shot a male in the act of singing this later song, and a few minutes later his mate. Their nest was evidently near as they scolded me with the usual Dendroica *chip* of alarm, and the abdomen of the female was denuded. These two birds were among a low growth of firs and pines and were shot without difficulty.

Geothlypis macgillivrayi. — Arrives about the middle of May and breeds rather commonly.

Geothlypis trichas occidentalis. — Arrives in May, and breeds sparingly. Common in the marshes in September.

Sylvania pusilla pileolata. — Taken occasionally in spring and autumn.

Setophaga ruticilla. — Abundant summer visitor, arriving about the last of May.

Anthus pensilvanicus. — Decidedly rare in spring, a few passing through about the middle of May. In the autumn they are very abundant, returning about the first of September, and a few lingering until early in November. At this season they frequent the dry, open prairies as well as the marshes about the lake, where they gather in large flocks.

Cinclus mexicanus. — Fairly common along suitable streams flowing into the lake.

Galeoscoptes carolinensis. — Common summer visitor.

Salpinctes obsoletus. — A pair found July 2, among the rocks on the summit of Mica Peak, where they were evidently nesting.

*Troglodytes aëdon parkmanii. — Breeds rather commonly. Mr. Brewster informs me that Fort Sherman birds are nearer to *parkmanii* than to *aztecus*.

Troglodytes hyemalis pacificus. — Rather common resident; found in suitable localities at all seasons. A series of skins sent to Mr. Brewster were pronounced by him to be "ultra typical," being darker than birds from the Pacific coast.

Cistothorus palustris paludicola. — Rare in autumn, among long grass and swamp willows in the marsh. None appear to breed at this end of the lake.

Certhia familiaris montana. — Abundant during winter. This is the only part of the Rocky Mountain region where I have found this species to be other than uncommon. During the month of April they gradually disappear, and only one was seen near the fort during the breeding season. It was not observed on Mica Peak, though it might easily have escaped notice; nor were any seen until about the middle of September, when they again appeared in company with Kinglets and Chickadees. While watching a Creeper one day at a distance of a few feet it suddenly flew and alighted on my leg for a second or two.

Sitta carolinensis aculeata. — The least common of the three species of Nuthatch, and usually associating with the Pygmy, but is by no means rare. Breeds rather sparingly about lake level and in the hills.

Sitta canadensis. — A common winter resident, breeding less plentifully near the fort and among the surrounding hills. Local specimens have unusually long bills.

Sitta pygmæa. — Probably the most abundant resident bird at Fort Sherman, in winter gathering in flocks with the other Nuthatches, Titmice, and Kinglets. Each year one or more pairs placed their nests within the weatherboarding of some of the buildings within the fort, entering through knotholes in the boarding. White-bellied Swallows, Wrens, and Western Bluebirds also did the same.

*** Parus atricapillus.** — A common resident. Its favorite breeding locality is among the swamp willows on the marsh, where a number of pairs gather each year, nesting in dead willow branches, sometimes scarcely three inches in diameter, and but little above the surface of the water.

In regard to the identification of this species Mr. Brewster writes me as follows:

"After carefully examining your series of Black-capped Titmice from Fort Sherman and comparing them with all the material contained in the National Museum, as well as in my own collection, I have come to the conclusion that they must be referred — at least provisionally — to *Parus atricapillus*. They are of practically the same size and proportion as our eastern bird, save in respect to the bill, which usually — but by no means invariably — is shorter and more conical in shape. In coloring, also, they resemble true *atricapillus* very closely, but as a rule they have less white on the wings and tail, more brownish on the sides, and deeper, clearer black on the crown and throat. These differences, however, are comparatively slight and inconstant, and do not seem to me to entitle the bird to separation under a distinctive name. It is awkward, of course, to cite it as *atricapillus*, but I see no alternative. One thing is certain, namely, that it is distinctly unlike either *occidentalis* or *septentrionalis*, despite the fact that it occupies a region lying between the respective ranges of these subspecies and far removed from the known western limits of the range of *atricapillus*."

Parus gambeli. — Abundant resident. Common in and about the fort in winter, most going to the adjacent hills to breed.

Parus rufescens. — This Chickadee is a fairly common resident in the vicinity of Fort Sherman, though more frequently seen in the hills than at lake level. Mr. Brewster informs me that local specimens are "identical in every respect" with skins from the coast of British Columbia.

Regulus satrapa olivaceus. — Common resident, especially in winter, most going up the surrounding hills to breed. A brood of fully fledged young seen at the fort on June 19.

Regulus calendula. — Arriving about the middle of April, this Kinglet is very abundant by the first of May. A large number pass through to the North, returning in September, but many remain to breed, and until the middle of June the song of the males may be heard in every direction.

Myadestes townsendii. — Not uncommon during the migrations, and I found one pair nesting near the summit of Mica Peak. It is an early migrant, arriving about the first of April, and I have taken a specimen as late as December 22.

* **Turdus fuscescens salicicola.** — Arriving about the twentieth of May, this Thrush is rather common among cottonwoods bordering the lake and river, where its sweet song may be heard towards evening. Nests found here were from two to seven feet above the ground, and in construction were essentially like those of the eastern form.

Turdus ustulatus swainsonii. — Breeds rather commonly about the lake and on Mica Peak up to the summit.

Merula migratoria propinqua. — Usually arrives during the last week in February and is abundant during the summer.

Hesperocichla nævia. — First noted during the first week of March when quite a number of males were found on the hillsides across the river, and also among the thickets under cottonwoods at the outlet of the lake. In 1896 the first were seen on April 3. They were generally flushed from the ground among dead leaves and alighting on a branch, uttered their peculiar *cluck* which, among the dense underbrush or young pines, often first attracted attention to the birds' presence. None were observed in autumn, but their habits are such that they might easily escape notice, and I have little doubt that some breed at no great distance from the fort.

Sialia mexicana bairdi. — Arrives late in February or early in March and is abundant during summer. Some specimens taken here are, in coloration, nearer *occidentalis* than *bairdi*.

Sialia arctica. — Usually arrives a few days later than the preceding species, and is less common at lake level, but is more generally distributed and more common in the hills. One pair nested on the sheltered corner of a rafter on the hospital porch.

NOTE. — Since most of this paper was put in type, I have received from Dr. C. Hart Merriam some unpublished field notes on Idaho birds made since the appearance of his report upon the subject. He kindly allows me to make the following extracts in order to bring the lists up to date:

Sphyrapicus thyroideus. — New to Idaho. Sawtooth City, Mr. Evermann. Near Coeur d'Alêne, August, 1895; Messrs. Bailey and Howell.
Sayornis saya.
Icteria virens longicauda. — Both recorded as common at Cœur d' Alêne. These three species are therefore to be added to the list of birds found in the vicinity of Fort Sherman.

I may say that early in 1897 about ten pairs of *Oreortyx pictus*, captured near Puget Sound, were liberated near the northern base of Mica Peak, and it was proposed to introduce the Bob White.

Printed by Libri Plureos GmbH in Hamburg, Germany